Dabney's Handbook
On
A Course in Miracles

A Practical Approach with Humor

Daya Devi-Doolin

Padaran Publications
Deltona, FL 32725

Dabney's Handbook
On
A Course in Miracles

A Practical Approach with Humor

Daya Devi-Doolin

Padaran Publications
Deltona, FL 32725

Dabney's Handbook on A Course in Miracles. Copyright 1988 by Daya Devi-Doolin. Second Edition 2022.

All rights reserved, including the right to reproduce the book, or any portion thereof, in any form without prior written permission of the Publisher, except for the inclusion of brief quotation in a review.

Portions reprinted by permission from A Course in Miracles Foundation for Inner Peace, Inc. 1975.

Library of Congress Catalog Card Number 88-92400

ISBN 978-1-877945-25-0

Cover Design by Daya Devi-Doolin
Edited Chris Doolin

Printed in the United States of America

This book is dedicated to the Light Bearers we all are; to my parents Sallie and Leon Brown Sr. who taught us only love; to my two sons Tyler and Joseph who are loving expressions of God to me; to my husband Chris who is the embodiment of truth and love and to I AM THAT I AM for my Eternal Blessings!

Other Books by Daya Devi-Doolin

Super Vita-Minds: How to Stop Saying I Hate You…To Yourself!

The Only Way Out Is In: The Secrets of the 14 Realms to Love, Happiness & Success

Americans Saving Ourselves Together: How to Thrive in the 21st Century

Grow Thin While You Sleep

Smile America

Yoga, Meditation and Spirituality for African American Community: If You Can Breathe, You CAN Do Yoga

I AM POWER

Hidden Manna: *A Dream Journey to Enlightenment*

Children's Books by Daya Devi-Doolin

Dormck

Dabney, Dormck and Wiggles' Slakaduman Adventure

Dormck and the Temple of the Healing Light

The Star of Aragon with Dabney, Dormck and Wiggles

Table of Contents

Acknowledgments	i
Foreword	iii
Part 1	1
Nothing Can Harm Me	3
"Why Nothing Seem to Go Right"	9
How to Identify the Illusions of Ego	13
I Am	19
How to Be Free of Ego	21
Forgiveness?	25
Trying to be God	51
Part 2	69
Poems inspired by ACIM	
Part 3 –	71
The 'Right One' All I Need to Know… Is Inside: *Pocket Bites* Affirmations and healing words for marriage and healthy relationships. The 'Right' One	78
The River of Life	85
The Unreal Door	98
Part 4- Believe You Have Received	101

Acknowledgments

I want to thank and acknowledge the guidance I've been given from the Holy Spirit all of my life. I want to thank Jesus the Christ within me for showing us that we too can transcend ego and limited thinking, for being my brother, friend, teacher and Savior. I thank God for opening my eyes so I can see beyond what I see, into the real world, the world of TRUTH.

I am ever so grateful for the Holy Bible, the Catherine Ponder books, books by Joseph Murphy, John Randolph Price, Ernest Holmes, Science of Mind Magazines, Unity School of Christianity books. I have received tremendous help from the Law of Life Volumes, Sondra Ray books, H. Emilie Cady, Wallace Wattles books and so many more too numerous to mention.

I'd like to thank the Foundation for Inner Peace for publishing A Course in Miracles, for Helen Schucman for being the Scribe and for Dr. William Thetford for transcribing Helen's notes so beautifully. I am grateful also for the permission granted to me to use the lessons here in my book.

I want to acknowledge my family, sons, and life-mate Chris Doolin for being loving and very supportive to me all our married life and in all I have been involved with. I have been very blessed by them.

I am thankful for this opportunity to be able to share this book of love with you and that you chose to share it with me.

Your friend and sister,
Daya Devi-Doolin

Foreword

The purpose of this handbook is to illustrate the concepts of A Course in Miracles in cartoon form, so it'd be fun and easy for young adults and people of all ages to grasp. Many have told me that the course was too difficult for them to understand or too complicated at this time for them to read. I have been led to show it can be otherwise.

Actually, there is nothing that is hard or easy, it just is. It only becomes hard or easy when we project our value of hard or easy onto a thing. We judge it to be or to have qualities of difficulty.

My part is to help draw the people who choose to be drawn into the TRUTH and show how they can change their lives by changing their minds about what they think they perceive.

When I was working in West Newton, Massachusetts for the Charles Water Products Company, I started receiving visions for a cartoon character who was to be called

Dabney. I drew funny office situations out of tense situations which I observed there. It caught everybody off guard and took away the tension because they never knew when they were to be featured in a Dabney cartoon situation.

I was later commissioned to do some work for them after I left the company. I didn't do much drawing from 1986 until 1988, when I distinctly heard that I must do Dabney cartoons that express A Course in Miracles lessons for daily living. This happened to me while I was working in Florida. I immediately received the pictures in my mind, effortlessly, concerning what to draw and the lessons that would best relate to the meaning of the cartoons. Before I would draw the next line, I would receive the image of how I was to use my pen to accomplish a foot, leg, shadowing, etc.

Included in this book are affirmations which I used to extend my learning of the truth, not just knowing what the truth is but by applying it to my life. I made a game of seeing how many ways I could extend the lessons either physically, verbally or spiritually. Poetry that I was inspired to write is included in this handbook as well.

As a Facilitator for A Course In Miracles along with my husband Chris, I shared many of these cartoons, affirmations and chapter summaries with the members of the study groups. It served to help clarify the various concepts being taught to us in the course.

I've included brief explanations and practical ways of identifying the ways ego tries to cover up your view, ego's purpose and goal, ego's games that keep you confused, worried, anxious and unforgiving.

In the drawings where I mention ACIM, it refers to A Course in Miracles. Where I have used the exact lesson from the workbook of ACIM, I have used quotes.

I hope you will enjoy the humor of the cartoons and the humor it places on life by looking at life through the eyes of the Christ, who is the embodiment of Joy and Love. I hope you will enjoy the lessons the cartoons display and not take life as you thought it to be, but as it truly is, full of love.

Our function here is forgiveness and with that knowledge, we can then see the miracles that are now "unseen", but would be everyday normal occurrences when our perception about what is changes to what IS. The course teaches that you can choose when you want to learn but you cannot choose the contents of what you are to learn. And, so It Is.

Your Sister in Light and Love,
Daya Devi-Doolin

Part 1

You can wait, delay, paralyze yourself or reduce your creativity almost to nothing, but you cannot abolish it.
-A Course in Miracles Text P. 9

Nothing Can Harm Me

Nothing outside yourself can harm you. Your fears create the havoc in your life, not anyone else or anything else. In reality, nothing can harm you. Nothingness is nothing. Fears are nothing-ness, they have no power but what you give to them. If you want to proclaim yourself as weak, a victim and your fears as strong, then you have free will to do so.

You can change the thoughts you wish to hold in your mind just as easily as you chose to hold onto the fear thoughts you selected and believed you had to hold onto.

I told a young teenager in counsel that it takes more energy to try to remember how much you hate your parents and all the mean things you think they "did" to you, than it does to be forgiving and loving towards them. They realized it took no pain, or struggle to love and that they had to do absolutely nothing to remember they loved their parents when they chose to be forgiving.

You selected to see your mother as unreasonable. You selected to see your dad, wife, brother, sister, friend as unloving. You selected to see whatever it is that makes you miserable. You also had to make up the reasons or justify in your mind why you had to believe you hate them for making you miserable. But you can choose to see with the eyes of Christ because you are Christ. You just forgot.

Each one of us is one with the Father, Son and the Holy Spirit. Each one of us has the same Christ consciousness as Jesus had; the enlightened consciousness that tells us I and the Father are one. Each one of us is the Mind, Idea and Action; God being Mind, Jesus Christ the Idea and the Holy Spirit the Action, the Law bearer and executive of the Will of God.

You have all the tools you need to change how you "look" at what you see. When you choose to see beyond your ego's perception of separation, you will see that you are one with your brother, one with Mind and that it is not possible to hate as you were told you had to do by ego.

"I can be hurt by nothing but my thoughts"…ACIM

When you release yourself from complaining and blaming, from condemning and judging yourself and others, you release yourself from the physical manifestation of your own judgment, not God's. But what you will receive from God is the Love that's been waiting for your recognition, your remembrance.

I've decided to discontinue condemning you and attacking you anymore Brubaker. I refuse to hold one last vestige of contempt toward you. You'll be getting that raise, with a bonus!

Why "Nothing" Seems to Go Right

Do you ever wonder why nothing ever goes "right" for you, or why your prayers never seem to get answered? Well, the answer is very simple. How much faith did you put into believing your prayer was already answered, or that your prayer would be answered?

By believing in the presence of the conditions that seem to appear in our lives, we make sure the conditions in our lives remain because we have not released them from our consciousness. You are affirming the truth of the conditions in your life and even though they are illusory again and again, they remain just as you see them in your "MIND".

You continue to hold onto the doubts, the fears, the conditions while "claiming" you want to be free of them. You can only be free if you choose to entertain the Holy Spirit as your only invited guest. The guests of the Holy spirit are peace, joy, happiness, certainty, substance, abundance, health, love, compassion, light and truth, etc. The guests of ego are doubt, disbelief, uncertainty, lack, depression, jealousy, hatred, unforgiveness, anger, condemnation, etc.

You cannot entertain the guests of ego and expect to have the guests of the Holy Spirit as well. You choose one and the other cannot be heard. When you release yourself from your laws, your limited beliefs, your fears that only you have manufactured, you will be able to hear the True Voice. You will be able to hear that your prayers have already been answered. The solution will be right in front of you as it always has been until you were ready to accept it and believe it.

Nope. The Holy Spirit is my only Invited Guest.

Wiggles, we love our neighbor as ourselves.

"Forgiveness is my only function here".
When we release ourselves from guilt, we are healed.

How to Identify the Illusions of Ego

Ego has invisible ways of condemning us which manifests our beliefs in the visible realm, whether we know what is going on or not. Since thoughts are never neutral, and are 'things', they form from divine substance all that we put our faith and belief into.

The ways in which we allow ego to condemn us are very subtle but no less true and powerful, because we have the POWER of God as our beingness. What we believe about ourselves in the inner (subconscious mind) must prove itself to us in the outer because of our faith in that belief.

For example, see if you recognize some of these thought patterns in your life:
- I'm too fat, too old…
- My arthritis, my asthma, my gout, my…
- I am getting wrinkles
- I am not strong anymore.
- My teeth and gums are getting diseased.

- I am not perfect.
- My mother and I always argue.
- My dad and I always argue.
- I can never lose weight.
- I'll never get married or find the right mate.
- I never look right.
- I am going to catch the flu.
- Am I going to catch the flu?
- Am I going to get Covid?

These thought patterns have no choice but to manifest that in which you believe to be true. You can deny the denial of truth about yourself by knowing that all that God has made is Holy. By affirming a lie about your holiness, you push the truth away from your consciousness and allow its unreal-ness to manifest for you. Even though the results of your thoughts do not make you happy, you are afraid to trust in the one thing that would make you happy. That is knowing you are whole and Holy throughout your entire being. You are believing in the idols that ego has provided you to believe in because you see yourself as not separate from ego, but from God.

Ego knows that when it has you involved in believing that you are in a state of lack consciousness and believing that God is nowhere to be found in your life, that you will not concentrate on knowing that God is speaking to you right now. In your involvement with doubt, you will not know that God is already providing you with the solution to your "problem" right this minute. All you need to do is BE STILL and LISTEN and you will hear I AM HERE. YOU ARE WHOLE! ALL IS WELL!

One time I was on a Mesa retreat for the weekend. We had to set up a small fire in the cake pan tin with twigs. I forgot fire burns and so I picked up a hot twig and let it go with my right fingers. My right thumb was on fire instantly. I drew a Reiki symbol on the roof of my mouth, then blew the symbol onto and across my thumb. I heard to ask the hostess of the Mesa retreat if she had any ointments for burns. I declined to ask for help right away. But I heard to ask again; this time I did and she did have a salve which contained plantain, bergamot, olive oil, chamomile and two other ingredients. She makes this for sale on her website. She was happy to get it for me. I used it right away. The pain was gone with Reiki and the salve immediately. Three weeks later, no scarring and still no pain. I would have caused myself anguish by not listening and so I am glad I did listen to that small quiet voice.

Early rising ritual before studying ACIM and after ACIM

Who am I to think I have the right to blaspheme my holiness as a Son of God?

I AM

Whatever we put our I AM consciousness to, whatever we believe in, the LAW of GOD which works through our subconscious level, is fulfilled. The purpose of our subconscious is to fill our lives with only good. It serves to fill our lives with what we put faith in, but we've turned it around believing in the negative realm so strongly that the LAW has to fulfill ITSELF in our lives according to the faith we put into our belief. It can be no other way.

There are many, many games ego will play with you if you choose to get caught up in them. See if you recognize any of these games in your life. These games keep you from knowing peace, harmony, abundance, love, faith in the TRUTH, while you have faith in FEAR (lack).

- I wonder what's going to go wrong today?

- What kind of disease will my child have?
- How will I survive if I give this up?
- How will I earn a living if I do what I want?
- Why am I always so poor?
- Why do I have so many bills?
- Why do I have to work so hard for so little?
- Why does he have more than I have?
- Why does my car always break down?
- Why do I always get into car accidents?

How to Be Free of Ego and Its Games?

Jesus' resurrection means that He transcended ego, not attacked it. By attacking, we make whatever lack we believe in real in our minds, so that we can never overcome by our own will. But we can transcend ego and take back the power given to us and it will remain as the nothing it was before we gave power to it to govern us. We do so by surrendering our "stubborn" will to the Will of the Holy Spirit, to be erased from our minds forever. We do this by releasing our hold onto the illusion of our "problem".

We must want to forgive ourselves for creating the problem. We have to want to forgive ourselves for holding onto the problem and we have to ask the Holy Spirit to erase all our error thoughts about the "problem" we thought we had. When we do this, we can then see the solution, which has always been there waiting for us to open and accept it. Be silent. Listen.

We must be willing to put our faith in the TRUTH instead of ILLUSION. We make illusion real by our faith in it, but it is not anything. We do not have to do anything when we put our faith in TRUTH. TRUTH just is. When we make our illusions real, we have to project our justifications onto them to prove to ourselves that what we feel and see must be the TRUTH because we believe it.

Who will you give your power to today, God or ego?

Forgiveness

Forgiveness is the tool we are given in this time and space existence to transcend that which we believe to be real, which is not. We have made it real in our minds and projected it onto others to keep them in a mental prison, away from our love, banned, so to speak, from receiving "our" love; but we don't realize that to keep another in prison, we must stay in prison with them to keep watch, don't we? With forgiveness, we don't have to do anything, keep guard, keep tense, keep hatred buried in every fiber, cell and tissue of our being. With forgiveness, we don't do anything else. Just Love. Only Love.

Before we studied ACIM, I always believed sickness was "out there". I just accepted it as TRUTH. I believed in sickness, pain, suffering because I had seen "proof" of its existence in my dad's life, my mother's life and others as I was growing up, including my own. I didn't realize the only way to be sick is to believe in its nothingness and give it power over you. I didn't realize that to be sick is to be experiencing guilt, or anger with oneself or another person, to feel justified that you are punishing yourself for holding onto grievances of one type or another.

Of course, if you knew what ego's purpose is for you, you would never accept those terms would you? No, you would not. Ego's purpose for you is death. That's its sole purpose. You think by trying to play as if you are God, meting out your own punishment for what you believe to be wrong, that when you do finally become ill, you blame it on God and ask "Why me God? What have I done to deserve this?" All the while you had been trying to judge yourself as you believe God would judge you, not knowing that God does not judge. It is only we ourselves who determine the punishment, be it carried out by ourselves or someone else. When we live according to the laws of ego, which we make up, we can never win at love because ego is not seeking love, only separation.

I'm making a list of things I'm forgiving you for. Can you think of anything else?

Since studying ACIM in conjunction with the Bible and other metaphysical books, I have learned to take back the power that I gave to sickness, pain and lack by removing my belief (faith) from them. By using an affirmation such as the one Myrtle Fillmore, founder of Silent Unity, used, I affirmed that "I do not believe in sickness. That I do believe in health because I am a child of God. I do not inherit sickness or suffering."

I learned that sickness is a form; a form of holding onto grievances, impure thoughts, unforgiving thoughts about persons or situations, feelings of helplessness or hopelessness. It's a belief that these invisible forms can hurt you or make you feel guilty for having these thought forms as your invited guests.

So, when we hold unforgiving thoughts about ourselves or anyone else, we justify in our own minds the reason why we cannot possibly love them or ourselves anymore. They are too awful to be forgiven and so am I for holding unforgiving thoughts about them or the situation. We believe we are split, or separate, from God and can make up our own rules about the LAW of LIFE. We cannot change the fact that God is Love, that God is the LAW of LIFE, that we are the creation of that LAW of LIFE and so we are love as well. Just because we put up a barrier to the door of God's love does not mean there is no door or that God's love does not exist.

In the Mind of God, there is nothing that we have done that needs to be forgiven because we are perfect, but it's for our own benefit that we forgive ourselves because we are the ones with a faulty misinterpretation of ourselves as being weak, unforgiving and unloving.

We can choose to worry or choose to TRUST…in God. Worry chains us to our fears, God breaks the links.

I am unlimited.

In God, there is no doubt.

I started giving my illusions over to the Holy Spirit.

Why can't she be the way I want her to be?

After ACIM – I forgive you for expecting me to be the way you want me to be.

"Nothing real can be threatened. Nothing unreal exists."

To give love does not require any conditions.

You choose how you will react to things around you with either love or fear.

Getting pleasure out of another one's misfortune hurts us as well because it torments us with guilt. This is not the way of attaining our real goal.

There can be no guilt. No blame.

You never know what a new day will bring!

Huh??????

I am grateful to the Universe for all things. I accept everything in my life as right.

How to stay happy Wiggles, lesson, 101.

Wiggles, would you make unreality real by giving power to it?

My patience with a child of God is my patience with myself.

"In my defenselessness my safety lies."

It's a struggle to hold onto unforgiving thoughts, fear, anger and guilt. With truth, there is nothing to do. It just is.

"The moment one takes cognizance of circumstances (illusions, appearance of lack) that moment she lets go of FAITH." – H. Emilie Cady

Things always go well when they are going well.

Wiggles, I think I'm beginning to hear that still, quiet voice.
Did you say you want to go out?

Trying to be God

When I tell God I believe He's doing something wrong, then I'm trying to be God, not BE God.

I Am Holy

Everything I do, say, think, feel and see is Holy, because I AM HOLY!

I CAN SEE

I baptize my eyes with strength and in the name of the Father, Son and Holy Ghost; all order and strength are now dispersed to all my centers. My eyes are blessed, my sight clean and pure. My eyes are bathed in pure substance of Divine Mind. All optic cells, nerves are renewed, opened, receptive to the Life Force now being received. All blockages are dissolved by the Holy Spirit within me and I am grateful. I believe I can see clearly.

Everywhere Cosmic Rays

I am filled, bathed, loved, protected, and blessed by Cosmic Rays. They penetrate, purify every cell of my eyes, my brain, my heart, my colon, my bladder, my reproductive organs, my legs, my teeth, gums, skin, organs, tissues, muscles, bones and blood. Cosmic rays filter out all negative Karma from my whole being and I KNOW I AM WHOLE! I am loved by these beautiful rays totally and completely.

Cosmic Rays

Cosmic rays from the Universe contain all the healing energy and light that I need to sustain and heal my thoughts, vision, and consciousness. I am truly grateful.

"Love created me like Itself."

"I can escape the world I see by giving up attack thoughts."

Start your day with a smile and get it over with.

God is and there is nothing else.
Holding onto to God is easy when I realize there is nothing else.

I am grateful to the Universe for all things.

I accept everything in my life as right!

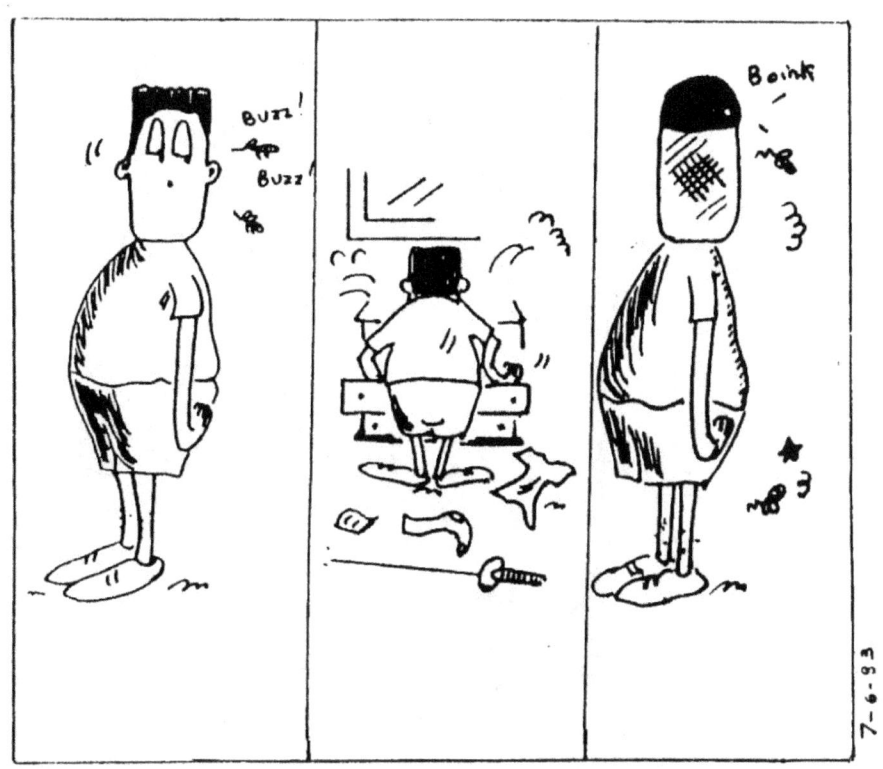

Our inner protection from false beliefs is there if we choose to find it.

Dad, if you could only learn to look past appearances, you wouldn't be so upset by my room.

"No one can escape from illusions unless she looks at them, for not looking is the way they are protected."

Idols (illusions) promise happiness, but only Truth delivers it.

You can always hear the Holy Spirit a second and a third time.

You could say, "There is another way of looking at this."

Do not help others to delude themselves in believing wrongly about themselves. Rather help them recognize their Oneness with God.

Remember you are in control of every situation unless you choose not to be.

My source of supply is my I AM PRESENCE. My PRESENCE has authority over conditions, circumstances, substance and produces my supply.

"Fear binds the world. Forgiveness sets it free." Would you rather be right or happy?
ACIM

Part 2

"When we give our love unconditionally to others with no expectations of return, the Love within us extends, expands and joins."– Gerald O. Jampolsky, M.D.

My Word

My word quickens the life in my twelve centers. My word expands these centers and they work on Universal levels. This is the second coming of Christ (subconscious awakening). The First Coming is the receiving of Truth into my conscious mind. I have faith in things invisible. For my back problem, I baptize and cleanse with my spiritual word every center. Baptism is cleansing. Baptism power cleanses all material thought. I am thankful.

I AM Grateful

I am grateful that all my illusions have been corrected. I am grateful my perceptions have been re-directed about my state of health by the Holy Spirit. I am grateful all my error thoughts have been erased!

Part 3
The 'Right One'

"Believe that ye have received and ye shall have."

-Joseph S. Benner-

Excerpt - All I Need to Know… Is Inside: *Pocket Bites*

In January of 1985, I made a little booklet to help myself and others. It was/is entitled, **All I Need to Know… Is Inside.** It was written to help keep me on the path of peace, harmony, health, abundance, and supply. The subtitle was ***Pocket Bites***, because you could put the booklet in your jacket pocket or pocketbook and take it out quickly to grab a few nuggets of truth. It was designed to put you back on track, as we sometimes get bumped off through ego's wanderings and accusations. I wrote this booklet after studying **ACIM** between 1983 to 1984.

Many of you know that Chris and I were homeless soon after we got married because a "friend" of ours, a member of our musical group, helped himself to the money we had saved up for our rent and future payment on a car and other needs. The details of this happening are in my second book, **The Only Way Out Is In: The Secrets of the 14 Realms to Love, Happiness & Success**! That took place in July of 1979. Spirit took care of us daily when we were playing music on the streets of Philadelphia. In 1983, we were given the gift of ACIM by a friend. We used the practical spiritual tools to help in daily living and bringing a new son, Joseph, into our lives and raising him.

Surrender Yourself and BE THERE

If we struggle with ego, yourself, you are never going to win. But as soon as you relinquish your struggle unto the hands of the Holy Spirit to undo the negative mental mass, you will be free. The negative mental mass will no longer compete for space in your subconscious, which controls the functioning of you bodily processes and organs and will eventually cause disease by doing so. These processes and organs will return to normal functioning once you get rid of the contentious mental climate. Surrender yourself to be there already.

    I was at a retreat where someone asked me why my left eye was crossed. I did not answer them. They soon became uncomfortable with the silence. Later that morning, the person came to me and apologized for hurting my feelings. My feelings had not been hurt. I gave them this response, "No one has the power to upset me, hurt me with their words or take away my faith or confidence in God. All good things are happening for me." They were stunned by my response. Before they walked away, I thanked them for their apology.

    Here are some *Pocket Bites* for you to quickly glance at, repeat to yourself aloud or quietly and firmly get back on track. The first one was personal for Chris and me.

- Divine love teaches us when to conceive. We are preparing to receive and conceive a child. We make great and loving parents. (By

keeping firm with our faith, we were gifted a baby boy whom we named Joseph after Joseph, the father of Jesus Christ). This affirmation was received in 1983 and Joseph came into our lives in 1994.
- I do not fight fear with fear. I meet it with a direct declaration: "God is the only Presence and the ONLY POWER and there is nothing to fear."
- Illusions, doubt, fear, or disbelief cannot occupy my mind because I choose to hear only the Holy Spirit.
- I affirm and am grateful that I am in the best financial situation possible that I can be in at this time. I am loving, firm but flexible in all that I do and take charge of my life through the Christ presence.
- All disease is manufactured in our own minds. My present conviction determines my future experience.
- I Am PRESENCE!
- I believe in the Law of Increase in the same manner that seeds deposited in the soil come forth multiplied 30-fold, 60-fold, 100-fold.

My thoughts come above the ground as conditions, experiences, and events. God governs the increase. His power is with my thoughts.
- Infinite Intelligence reveals to me all I need to KNOW!
- I AM THAT I AM. In order that I might BE, I KNOW I AM THAT.
- I know my subconscious mind is a bank which multiplies and magnifies whatever I deposit. I make these thoughts real by feeling the reality of them. I sow Godlike thoughts and these wonderful seeds of success and prosperity will automatically bring forth a success harvest NOW! Thank You Father! Hallelujah.
- I can do all things through the God Power within me. I AM a wonderful and successful singer/songwriter, author and business woman. I AM a child of God and what is true of HIM is true of me.
- I am in love with music and it reveals all its secrets to me. I am in love with the Universe and it reveals all its secrets to me.

- Be Still and KNOW that I AM GOD.
- I Am truly thankful because I have found God in the midst of me. He delivers me from all my fears.
- All the thoughts entertained by me conform to harmony, peace and goodwill.
- God is guiding me now. His love fills my soul. He inspires me and illumines my pathway in life. I radiate love and good will to all. Divine Law and order governs my life at all times.
- I avoid ups and downs by realizing that Divine Law and order govern my life and that God speaks, acts, thinks and directs all my undertakings!
- All my possessions and investments are watched over by God and I dwell constantly in the Secret Place.
- I decree my own security, peace, joy and health through the Laws of my Mind.
- God restores my soul and thought life. I have chosen to dwell mentally and spiritually with God all the days of my life.

- I AM always poised, balanced and calm for I know that God always will reveal to me the perfect solution to all my needs. I shall not want for anything. I hear the melody of God's whisper.
- I give thanks for the perfect harmonious solution which takes place through the wisdom of the All-wise One.

Affirmations and healing words for marriage and healthy relationships. The 'Right' One

I have shared the following information with my two adult sons. That is the idea that basically the Universe loves to provide us with everything we believe we desire. Whether good or bad, we ultimately get what we believe in. If we believe we lack, it must provide us with more lack. If we claim we are lonely, lack friends, are alcoholic or addicted, it provides more reality of this for us easily and effortlessly. Everything we claim to have sinks into our subconscious and we are given more of that "thing" that we focus and believe in.

So instead of asking for more of what we don't want, loneliness for example, let's focus on the "have" reality, the I AM of that reality of what we do want. One example is, I noticed this process in action when I visited my in-laws. My future nephew in-law was at a rehearsal dinner for Chris' nephew and his bride to be. He was standing next to Chris' niece. Being intuitive, I could hear him say in his mind, "I AM HER HUSBAND!" Nobody heard him but me. I said to myself, "Wow! Did I just hear him say he's her husband?" (I was asking my higher Self). About a half hour later, the couple moved up to my left side at the table, still standing and talking with us up at that end. Now into my left ear, he said again, "I AM HER HUSBAND!" Again, I go "Wow! I did hear him say that!" He had not asked her to marry him at that time. It was his secret mantra to God and me.

He was speaking from the Realm he desired to be in, a new state of mind. I told my sister in-law that night about what I had heard. She did say that he had not asked her to marry him. At the reception of their wedding two years later, she said to me, "You were right Daya. I remember you told me he was her husband."

If you were looking for the perfect mate in your life, you might follow a script similar to the one below to create the positive visualization to set the ball in motion.

See yourself writing it out and telling yourself what you want to experience in the present moment. "I just met that perfect one for me. She loves God above everything else. She loves herself and loves me very much. She's a happy person, a fun person and she loves giving to others. She only has kind words to offer to anyone and makes them feel good. I love being around her. She's fun, loving, kind, honest and trustworthy. She would be great as a mother. She is adventuresome, doesn't mind taking risks and loves sharing her ideas with me. She loves giving me things and surprising me. She doesn't drink and has no interest in abusing drugs. I see she is not obsessed about her body, hair, money, or material things in general. She is a very clean person and I love her aroma. My friend is wise, funny and loves to travel. She sees travelling as a way to enrich her life and mine. She has a wonderful job and has ideas that might lead her to greater prosperity someday because she is unique in the way she thinks. I am always happy to be around her because she is not a complainer or negative person. I know God put her here for me so we can help each other to grow together spiritually."

You would continue in this vein with as much detail as needed to move the needle and begin the wheels turning in your subjective self (subconscious) to go out and make this a reality for you in the material dimension. Enliven these words with feeling and emotion to make an impression on your subconscious mind. So, your job is to place yourself in the Realm of being with the 'Right' one for you by giving the Universe permission to usher him/her to you.

One word of caution though. Do not be that person like the woman on the beach who is standing with her child when a rogue wave sweeps in and carries him off into the deep ocean. She frantically cries out to God to help save her child. Soon she sees an albatross flying by off the coast who dives into the ocean and pulls out her child, flies over in her direction and gently deposits him on the beach. She looks up at the sky and calls out, "He had a hat," referring to the child's hat lost during this incident. The universe will invariably respond to your visioning in ways slightly unexpected, so be flexible and open for your greatest good. We often end our affirmative statements with "Amen or So It Is!" Do you really know what is best for you, better than your Creator/Higher Self.

Here is your homework:
- These are the things I am doing to prepare myself for attracting my ideal mate or husband/wife.
- I had a beautiful wedding ceremony with my husband/wife. Here are the photos of our setting.

- I am so thankful the Universe matched me up perfectly with an understanding, loving, fun, adventuresome, dependable and trusting partner.
- The wedding band I received is very beautiful. Here is a photo of it.
- Every evening I now set the table up for two with plates, forks, knives and spoons.
- I like the matching bathroom towels we received as wedding gifts (go buy them now).
- My partner loves everything about me. He/she says I am unique.
- I have nothing to complain to the Universe about my partner.
- I am emotionally, physically, spiritually, and lovingly attracted to my mate and vice versa. So, BE IT! All my past relationships are healed, forgiven and left behind. So Grateful.
- I went to my jewelry store and picked out my wedding ring or engagement for my intended bride. This is a photo of what it looks like.

- I decluttered my master bedroom to make room for my new partner to have space for his/her clothes.
- Through God's grace, I stopped drinking alcohol on regular basis.
- Through God's Grace, I know truth is my only ally.
- Through God's Grace, being untruthful cannot get me anywhere.
- I no longer need to use external means such as smoking or drinking to de-stress. The tools I use for de-stressing, to worry less and be less anxious are within me through the Holy Spirit. I TRUST more and I realize that ALL IS WELL!
- I no longer need to hate myself for not being married.
- It's easy for me to be loved and to love. I am Love created like itself.
- What are the negative habits I am willing to give up in order to meet what God has waiting for me.

- The thoughts I have concerning being married are no longer needed if I don't feel good thinking them. I am ready to BE who I AM meant to be. I deserve the best from life and I deserve to give the best of myself at all times.

The River of Life
(The Holy Spirit)
Daya Devi-Doolin

Inspired by Author Joseph S. Benner of The Impersonal Life

I am the Reservoir
For the River of Life
It's job, to fill me up.
If I allow holes to form
Such as doubts, or disbeliefs,
Then it cannot remain with me very long.
It cannot help me to sing a new song.,
Dance a new dance,
Wear a new name or see
My new face.

I thought life was rough until I let the rough part go.

"In ego, there is only confusion, condemnation and attack, In God there is no conflict."

"I will not allow my world to obscure my Christ vision."

There is another way of looking at this.

"I place the future in the hands of God"
ACIM-W; p. 194

Every opportunity gives us a chance to teach what we are, LOVE.

I AM NOT LOST
Daya Devi-Doolin Copyright 1989

My Lord loves me.
My Lord is loving me.
My Lord is loving me now.
My Lord is love.
My Lord and I are One.
I love my Lord.
I have always loved my Lord.
I will always love my Lord.
I and my Lord are One.
I am God's love.
I am wonderful.
I am spiritual.
I am special.
I am not forgotten.
I am not lost

I AM Grateful
Daya Devi-Doolin

I am grateful that all my illusions have been corrected. I am grateful my perceptions have been re-directed about my state of health by the Holy Spirit. I am grateful all my error thoughts have been erased!

"Love waits on welcome, not time."
ACIM

"I am at home. Fear is the stranger here."
ACIM

What Will Take the Place of Fear?
Inspired by A Course in Miracles, – Daya Devi-Doolin 1989

The things the world thinks that it sees
Holds dear the images it sees
Through darkened glass
It grabs on tight with gripping nails
To fears, in nightly fright.
Fear of death and fear of loss;
Fear of fear itself;
Fear of love and fear of hate;
And Fear of what just seems.
The things the world thinks that it sees
Makes lines seem solid here,
But the darkened glass when once removed
Will reveal the Love of Him
And the Light obscured but for a time
Will take the place
Of
Fear.

The Unreal Door
Daya Devi-Doolin, Copyright 1989
Inspired by Ruby Nelson, "The Door of Everything"

Who sees the unreal door
But the one who wants to hold
The vision of illusion?
Who sees the unreal door
But the one who believes he is alone?
Who sees the unreal door
But the one who believes only in his truth?
The unreal door
Keeps out love.
It keeps out patience too.
It keeps out gratitude and joy and truth.
The unreal door
Allows us to believe a lie.
There is only one door,
The Door of Everything.
But until one walks through
The veil of the unreal door,
He will continually keep it shut tight,

Not knowing it doesn't exist at all.
The only thing the unreal door can promise
Is that it will delay
Our walking through
The Door of Everything.

You cannot have any bad days when you are connected with God.

Part 4

"Believe that ye have received and ye shall have."

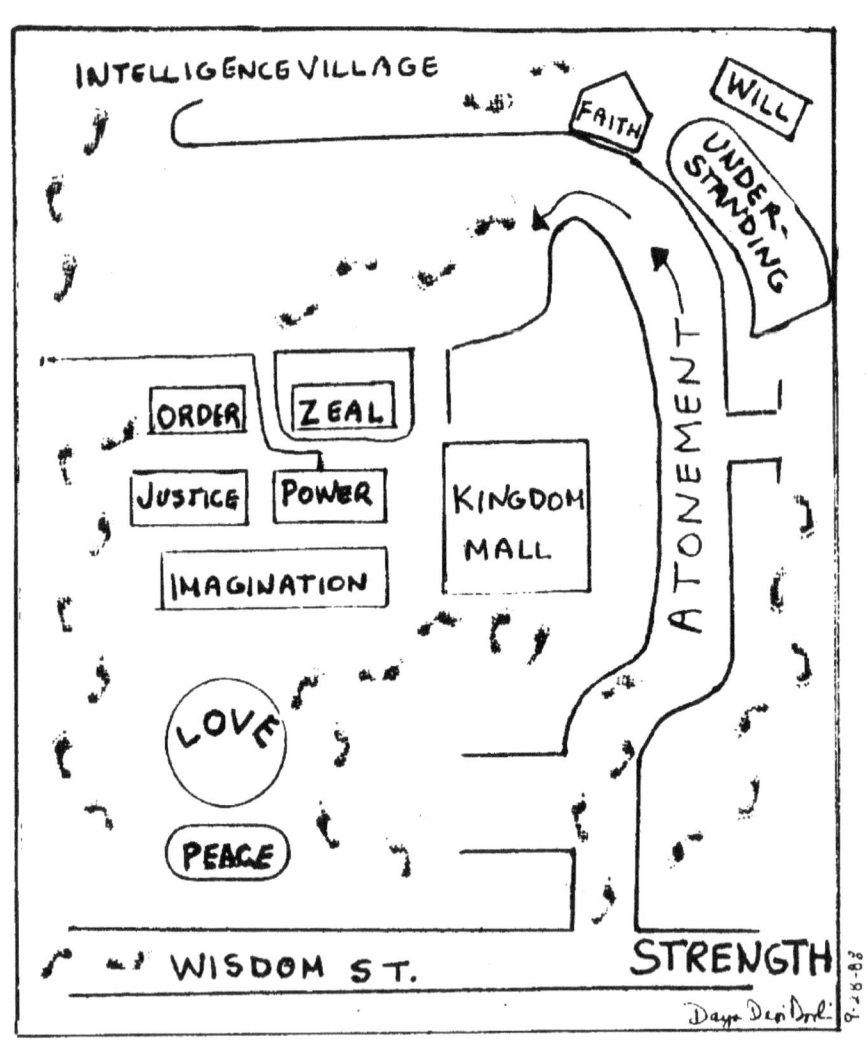

Let Jesus Christ guide you there.

In Conclusion, just a reminder from Dabney, remember when you release yourself from complaining, blaming, condemning, judging, attacking yourself and others, you release yourself from the physical manifestation of your judgment, not God's, because God does not judge. But what you will receive from Him is the Love that's been waiting for your recognition, your remembrance.

We must realize that our function here, is forgiveness. With that knowledge, we can then see the miracles that we previously thought were not there. We must change from seeing only what we want to see, to what God has in store for us to see. When we start doing that, we will be seeing only love. We will be teaching ONLY LOVE and nothing else will matter.

Recommended Books

A Course in Miracles, published by the Foundation for Inner Peace, Tiburon, CA 1975. The Text, Workbook & Manual remind you that you are perfect and that you are Love. It teaches you how to change your thought pattern from one of fear, lack, attack, blame and how to look at what you perceive and look beyond it to the truth of all things. It reminds you that you already know how to forgive but have forgotten by choice. You learn to release and let go of ego and enjoy doing it, because you know that is where your peace lies.

How I Used Truth by H. Emilie Cady. Unity School Christianity Publisher, 1950. Lee's Summit, Mo. This book deals with how to apply the principles of Truth to our lives and how to prove it for ourselves.

Law of Life, Vol.,1 & 2 by A.D. Luk, A.D. Luk Publications, CO. 1960. These volumes give an understanding of fundamental truths, universal law and principles, with practical application. They help us to accept our own God Presence and to trust our I AM PRESENCE.

Love is Letting Go of Fear by Gerald G. Jampolsky, M.D. Bantam Books, NY. 1979. This will help you to realize that you have a choice in selecting peace or conflict for yourself. A Course in Miracles is the source of the lessons contained in it. A national bestseller of his is "Goodbye to Guilt".

Pray and Grow Rich by Catherine Ponder, Parker Publishing Co. 1968. She has many books including *The Dynamic Laws of Prosperity*, *The Dynamic Laws of Healing*, *Prosperity Secrets of the Ages*. Her books are Christian oriented and metaphysical in nature.

The Impersonal Life by Joseph S. Benner, DeVorss & Co., 1941. It makes clear the way out of all your problems. It explains wisdom, strength, and shows you that you already know how to bring peace, health and the abundance of all your heart's desires. We are taught to BE STILL and KNOW THAT I AM GOD. It's telling your ego that you are GOD and not it. Another book by Benner is called THE WAY TO THE KINGDOM.

The Only Diet There Is by Sondra Ray, Celestial Arts, 1981. "It's about going all the way, looking at your problems, the reason for them, the surrendering of them to the Holy Spirit and releasing yourself totally. To love yourself and those around you." Sondra Ray also has other books, one is a Summary to A Course in Miracles. It beautifully summarizes the Course and has practical applications as well for you.

The Twelve Powers of Man by Charles Fillmore. Unity School of Christianity Publishers, Unity Village, MO. This book deals "with forces that function below and above the field of the conscious mind, the subconscious mind and the superconscious mind."

Super Beings by John Randolph Price. Quartus Foundation, 1981. Austin, TX. He "invites you to move up to the level of mastery." It's a "How to" book…how to be well spiritually, mentally, emotionally, physically, and financially so you will be ready in consciousness to take your place in the new world of the Superbeings." Other books are the Abundance Book (40 Day Prosperity Plan) a 60 Day non-Human Plan and many more books.

Super Vita-Minds: How to Stop Saying I Hate You…To Yourself, Padaran Publications 1997. A book on how to feed the subconscious mind with super love thoughts that erase the race consciousness thought patterns with the guidance of the Holy Spirit. Daya Devi-Doolin's others books include Hidden Manna (A Dream Journey to Enlightenment), The Only Way Out Is In:

The Secrets of the 14 Realms to Love, Happiness & Success, Grow Thin While You Sleep, I AM POWER, Americans Saving Ourselves Together in How to Thrive in the 21st Century, Smile America, Yoga, Meditation and Spirituality for the African American Community: If You Can Breathe, You CAN Do Yoga and books that include metaphysical topics, fun and adventure for children.

Other Books by Daya Devi-Doolin

Super Vita-Minds: How to Stop Saying I Hate You…To Yourself! (https://www.amazon.com/Daya-Devi-Doolin-Vita-Minds-1997-12-16-Paperback/dp/B002IUK8SO)

The Only Way Out Is In: The Secrets of the 14 Realms to Love, Happiness & Success (https://www.amazon.com/-/es/Daya-Devi-Doolin/dp/1877945145)

Americans Saving Ourselves Together: How to Thrive in the 21st Century (https://www.amazon.com/Americans-Saving-Ourselves-Together-Century/dp/1877945161)

Grow Thin While You Sleep (https://www.amazon.com/dp/187794520X)

Smile America (https://www.amazon.com/dp/1877945188)

Yoga, Meditation and Spirituality for African American Community: If You Can Breathe, You CAN Do Yoga (https://www.booksamillion.com/p/Yoga-Meditation-Spiritual-Growth-African/Daya-Devi-Doolin/9781937269463)

I AM POWER
(https://www.amazon.com/dp/B07RCVQTWK)

Hidden Manna: *A Dream Journey to Enlightenment*

Children's Books by Daya Devi-Doolin

Dormck

Dabney, Dormck and Wiggles' Slakaduman Adventure

Dormck and the Temple of the Healing Light

The Star of Aragon with Dabney, Dormck and Wiggles

Journaling Page

www.ingramcontent.com/pod-product-compliance
Lightning Source LLC
LaVergne TN
LVHW051842080426
835512LV00018B/3019